The Battle of Gettysburg: 46 Fascinating Facts For Kids

Kevin Ashmole

This book is just one of a series of "Fascinating Facts For Kids" books. For more fascinating facts about people, history, animals, and much more, please visit:

www.fascinatingfactsforkids.com

Contents

A Country at War

1. In the mid-19th century the United States of America was a country divided, and the main reason was the issue of slavery. For more than 200 years people had been brought from Africa against their will, and forced to work long hours on southern farms and plantations for no pay.

Slaves working on a plantation

2. The economy of the southern United States depended on the free labor provided by slaves, but the northern states thought that slavery was wrong and wanted to abolish it.

3. In 1860, Abraham Lincoln – a northern politician who was strongly opposed to slavery – was elected president of the United States. None of the southern states had voted for Lincoln, and they were so angry that they threatened to leave the United States and form their own country.

Abraham Lincoln

4. In the weeks following Lincoln's election victory, eleven southern states separated from the North and joined together to form the

Confederate States of America. The Confederates elected a president of their own, Jefferson Davis.

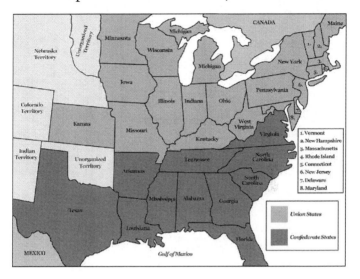

The northern (Union) and southern (Confederate) states

5. Lincoln refused to accept the existence of the Confederate States of America, arguing that it had been against the law for the southern states to break away from the North. Tensions between the North and South were now so great that it looked like war might break out.

6. Lincoln was desperate to avoid a war between the northern states - which were called the "Union" – and the Confederates, but on April 12, 1861, Confederate troops attacked a Unionist fort, Fort Sumter, at Charleston, South Carolina. The American Civil War had begun.

The attack on Fort Sumter

7. The American Civil War would last for four years and claim more than 600,000 lives. Many battles took place in different parts of the country – mainly in the South - but the most famous and bloodiest battle took place in July 1863, at the small town of Gettysburg, Pennsylvania.

General Lee's Plan

8.   During the first two years of the Civil War, the Confederate and Union Armies fought battle after battle all over the South. The Confederate strategy was to defend its territory, while the Union's goal was to capture southern cities and destroy the Confederate Army.

9.   In May 1863, the Confederate Army, under the command of General Robert E. Lee, defeated the Unionists at the Battle of Chancellorsville in northern Virginia. It was a stunning victory and the Confederates were in high spirits and full of confidence.

General Robert E. Lee

10. Following the victory at Chancellorsville, General Lee devised a plan which he hoped would bring an end to the war. He would march his Army into enemy territory to take on the Union, hoping that beating the Union Army on its own soil would break the Northerners' spirit and convince them to give up the fight.

11. Lee's Army entered the northern state of Pennsylvania in late June 1863. The Union Army had heard reports of Confederate movement and they set off in pursuit. The two Armies would meet at the town of Gettysburg on the morning of July 1.

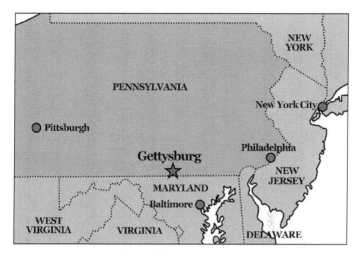

12. Gettysburg was a small town in farming country with a population of just 2,400. It was surrounded by hills, ridges, and valleys, making it the ideal location for a 19th-century battle. It was here that more than 165,000 soldiers would fight in the bloodiest battle of the war.

Day One

13. The first shots of the Battle of Gettysburg were fired early in the morning of July 1. A small group of Confederate soldiers entered the town from the west, and were fired on by Union soldiers under the command of General John Buford.

General John Buford

14. The fighting quickly escalated as General Lee and the Union Army commander, General George G. Meade, sent more soldiers into Gettysburg. Soon 25,000 Union soldiers and 20,000 Confederates were engaged in heavy fighting.

General George G. Meade

15. More and more Confederate soldiers poured into Gettysburg from the north and west, and at around 3.00 p.m. they launched a huge attack on the enemy. The Union forces were driven back through the streets of Gettysburg, suffering huge casualties. The survivors managed to retreat to areas of high ground to the south of the town - Cemetery Hill, Cemetery Ridge, and Culp's Hill. There, they prepared for another Confederate attack.

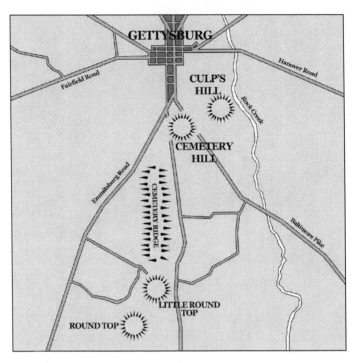

16. General Lee knew the importance of occupying high ground, and he ordered General Richard Ewell to attack Cemetery Ridge and take it for the Confederates. But Ewell didn't carry out the order, believing his men were too exhausted from the day's battle.

17. The first day of the Battle of Gettysburg had been devastating for the Union Army, with 10,000 men killed, wounded, or captured. But they had taken important high-ground positions, and more Union troops would be arriving the next day.

Day Two

18. By the second day of the Battle of Gettysburg, both Armies were at full strength – 94,000 soldiers on the Union side, and 72,000 Confederates. On the morning of July 2, General Lee decided to attack Union troops at Culp's Hill, and also on the west and south sides of Cemetery Ridge in an attempt to crush the Union Army.

19. The Union troops were spread out for over four miles (6.5 km) and it took until the middle of the afternoon for the Confederates to get their soldiers and cannons into position. Meanwhile, the Union Army was able to prepare for the coming attack.

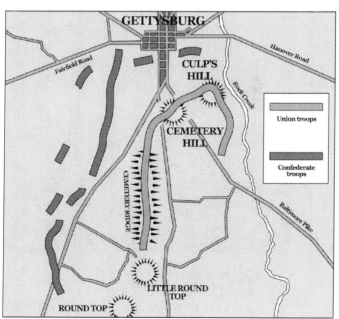

20. General Daniel Sickles was in charge of a group of Union soldiers toward the south of Cemetery Ridge, but he thought that his position was weak. Against the orders of General Meade he moved his men to higher ground, half a mile (0.8 km) closer to the Confederate Army.

21. General Sickles had put his men in a vulnerable position, and when the Confederate attack started at 4.00 p.m. the Union troops suffered heavy losses in the fierce fighting that followed. Sickles himself was hit by a cannonball which shattered his right leg. He was carried from the battlefield to a first aid station where his leg had to be amputated.

22. To the south of Cemetery Ridge was a hill known as Little Round Top, which General Sickles' actions had left unprotected. If either Army could capture Little Round Top, they would have a big advantage, being able to fire down on enemy troops.

Little Round Top today

23. General Meade sent soldiers to Little Round Top, and after heavy fighting with Confederate troops they succeeded in capturing the hill. The Confederates attacked Little Round Top again and again, but they were unable to capture it. The battle for Little Round Top was one of the Union's most important victories at Gettysburg.

24. While the fighting was going on at Cemetery Ridge and Little Round Top, Confederate troops launched an attack further north at Culp's Hill, under the command of General Richard S. Ewell.

General Richard S. Ewell

25. Culp's Hill was steep and covered in boulders, and the Confederate progress was slow and difficult. The Union Army was able to hold off the Confederates and prevent the capture of the hill. As darkness fell, the Confederates positioned themselves at the bottom of Culp's Hill and waited for morning, when they would try to catch the Union Army by surprise with an attack at dawn.

Day Three

26. The surprise attack by the Confederates at Culp's Hill never came. Instead, at 4.30 a.m. Union soldiers opened fire on the Confederate troops. The fighting lasted nearly seven hours, and by 11.00 a.m. the Union Army had driven the Confederates back and held on to Culp's Hill.

Union troops on Culp's Hill

27. General Lee wanted to finish off the Union Army and decided to gamble by launching an all-or-nothing attack. Shortly after 1.00 p.m. more than 150 heavy guns and cannons began a massive two-hour bombardment of Cemetery Ridge.

28. At 3.00 p.m. the cannons stopped, and 12,500 Confederate soldiers, under the command of General George Pickett, began the one-mile (1.6 km) march across open fields toward the Union Army.

General George Pickett

29. As the Confederates got closer to Cemetery Ridge they became the perfect target. Union troops opened fire and were able to mow down huge numbers of Confederate soldiers.

Union soldiers on Cemetery Ridge

30. The Confederate attack, which became known as "Pickett's Charge," lasted for an hour and was a total disaster. Around 7,000 Confederate soldiers were killed or wounded, and the survivors were forced to retreat back to Confederate positions. The Battle of Gettysburg was over – General Lee's gamble had failed and it was the Union Army that was victorious.

Aftermath

31. On July 4, the day after the battle, General Lee waited for an attack from the Union Army, but it never came. General Meade's men were exhausted after three days of hard fighting.

32. General Lee knew that the Battle of Gettysburg was lost, and he and his Army began the long retreat back to the South. A wagon train that stretched for seventeen miles (27 km) carried the thousands of wounded Confederate soldiers back home.

The type of wagon used in the Confederate retreat

33. The news of the Union victory at Gettysburg had reached president Lincoln, and he wanted General Meade to chase after the retreating Confederate Army to finish it off and bring an end to the war.

34. But Meade was too cautious and chose to rest his troops and wait for fresh supplies to be brought in. Allowing the Confederate Army to return home where it could build up its strength meant that the war would go on for another two years.

35. General Lee blamed himself for the defeat at Gettysburg and offered his resignation to the Confederate president, Jefferson Davis, but the offer was refused. General Meade also offered his resignation to President Lincoln, but Lincoln forgave his general for the failure to finish off the Confederate Army, and Meade stayed in charge of the Union Army for the rest of the war.

The Gettysburg Address

36. At the end of the Battle of Gettysburg, thousands of dead Union and Confederate soldiers lay across the hills and fields surrounding the town. Many had been hurriedly buried in shallow graves and others had been left where they fell.

Dead Union soldiers

37. The people of Gettysburg felt that the dead soldiers should be properly buried, and they drew up plans to build a cemetery on Cemetery Hill, just to the south of the town. The cemetery was finished in November 1863, and President Lincoln was invited to speak at the opening ceremony.

38. On November 19, 20,000 people gathered at the new cemetery to hear the president speak. He wasn't the only speaker – Edward Everett, a distinguished politician and one of the country's finest speechmakers, spoke for nearly two hours before it was the president's turn.

39. President Lincoln's speech was just 272 words in length and lasted less than three minutes. But despite being so short it has become one of the most famous speeches in American history. Lincoln spoke movingly about the reasons why the war was so important for the freedom and equality of everyone in America. It is known today as the "Gettysburg Address."

40. The American Civil War ended in the spring of 1865 with a Union victory, and the country began the process of re-uniting as one nation. President Lincoln was assassinated just five days after the war's end, but his leadership during four years of bloody conflict and his opposition to slavery has seen him go down as one of the great American presidents.

Assorted Battle of Gettysburg Facts

41. The Battle of Gettysburg was the deadliest battle of the Civil War and is the largest battle ever to have been fought on American soil. Around 4,500 Confederates lost their lives and 20,000 were wounded. There were more than 3,000 Union deaths and around 14,500 wounded.

42. The bombardment of Cemetery Ridge by Confederate cannons, which took place before Pickett's Charge on the last day of the battle, produced the loudest man-made noise ever to have been heard in North America. The sound was so loud that it could be heard in Harrisburg, Pennsylvania – forty miles (64 km) from the scene of the battle.

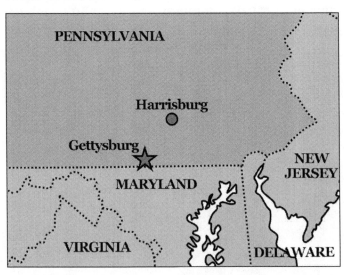

43. When General Daniel Sickles had his leg amputated on the second day of the battle, he didn't want the doctors to throw his limb away. He kept the bones, and after the war he put them in a coffin-shaped box and donated them to a museum in Washington, D.C. For many years he visited his leg on the anniversary of the battle.

44. Although General Robert E. Lee was born in the southern state of Virginia, he trained for the Army at West Point, the famous military academy in the northern state of New York. Shortly before the Civil War started, President Lincoln asked Lee to take command of the Union Army, but he turned the president down because he didn't want to fight against his fellow Southerners.

45. The only civilian to die at the Battle of Gettysburg was twenty-year-old Jennie Wade. On the morning of July 3, Jennie was baking bread at her sister's house, when she was hit through the heart by a stray bullet, killing her instantly.

46. Although the Gettysburg Address has become one of America's most famous speeches, it wasn't received enthusiastically at the time, with little applause coming from the crowd. President Lincoln himself called it "a flat failure," but souvenir copies of the speech were soon being printed, and the 272 words became part of American history.

Lincoln's Words at Gettysburg

The Gettysburg Address - November 19, 1863

"*Four score and seven years ago our fathers brought forth on this continent a new nation, conceived in liberty, and dedicated to the proposition that all men are created equal.*

Now we are engaged in a great civil war, testing whether that nation, or any nation so conceived and so dedicated, can long endure. We are met on a great battlefield of that war. We have come to dedicate a portion of that field, as a final resting place for those who here gave their lives that that nation might live. It is altogether fitting and proper that we should do this.

But, in a larger sense, we cannot dedicate, we cannot consecrate, we cannot hallow this ground. The brave men, living and dead, who struggled here, have consecrated it, far above our poor power to add or detract.

The world will little note, nor long remember what we say here, but it can never forget what they did here. It is for us the living, rather, to be dedicated here to the unfinished work which they who fought here have thus far so nobly advanced.

It is rather for us to be here dedicated to the great task remaining before us - that from these honored dead we take increased devotion to that cause for which they gave the last full measure of devotion - that we here highly resolve that these dead shall not have died in vain - that this nation, under God, shall have a new birth of freedom - and that government of the people, by the people, for the people, shall not perish from the earth."

Illustration Attributions

Cover
Ron Cogswell, CC BY 2.0
<https://creativecommons.org/licenses/by/2.0>
via Wikimedia Commons

Slaves working on a plantation
New-York Historical Society, Public domain, via
Wikimedia Commons
{{PD-US}}

Abraham Lincoln
Soerfm, CC BY-SA 3.0
<https://creativecommons.org/licenses/by-
sa/3.0>, via Wikimedia Commons

The attack on Fort Sumter
Currier & Ives. Uploaded by Christophe Cagé
12:52, 6 September 2006 (UTC), Public domain,
via Wikimedia Commons
{{PD-US}}

General Robert E. Lee
Julian Vannerson, Public domain, via Wikimedia
Commons
{{PD-US}}

General John Buford
Brady National Photographic Art Gallery
(Washington, D.C.), photographer, Public
domain, via Wikimedia Commons
{{PD-US}}

General George G. Meade
Library of Congress, Public domain, via
Wikimedia Commons
{{PD-US}}

Gettysburg map (Facts 15 & 19)
Map by Hal Jespersen, www.posix.com/CW, CC
BY 3.0
<https://creativecommons.org/licenses/by/3.0>
via Wikimedia Commons

Little Round Top today
Wilson44691
https://creativecommons.org/publicdomain/zer
o/1.0/deed.en
https://creativecommons.org/publicdomain/zer
o/1.0/legalcode

General Richard S. Ewell
Library of Congress Prints and Photographs
Division, Public domain, via Wikimedia
Commons
{{PD-US}}

Union troops on Culp's Hill
Edwin Forbes, Public domain, via Wikimedia
Commons
{{PD-US}}

General George Pickett
{{PD-US}}

Made in the USA
Coppell, TX
12 December 2023

25987197R00020